Nine
Fruits
of the
Spirit

A Bible Study on Developing Christian Character

Strand

New Leaf Press

A Division of New Leaf Publishing Group

First printing: June 1999
Third printing: September 2009

Copyright © 1999 by New Leaf Press. All rights reserved. No part
of this book may be used or reproduced in any manner whatsoever
without written permission of the publisher, except in the case of
brief quotations in articles and reviews. For information write:
New Leaf Press, P.O. Box 726, Green Forest, AR 72638.

ISBN-13: 978-0-89221-464-8
ISBN-10: 0-89221-464-3
Library of Congress Number: 99-64015

Cover by Janell Robertson

Printed in China

Please visit our website for other great titles:
www.newleafpress.net

For information regarding author interviews, please contact the
publicity department at (870) 438-5288.

Contents

Introduction

There is an ancient story out of the Middle East which tells of three merchants crossing the desert. They were traveling at night in the darkness to avoid the heat of the day. As they were crossing over a dry creek bed, a loud attention-demanding voice out of the darkness commanded them to stop. They were then ordered to get down off their camels, stoop down and pick up pebbles from the creek bed, and put them into their pockets.

Immediately after doing as they had been commanded, they were then told to leave that place and continue until dawn before they stopped to set up camp. This mysterious voice told them that in the morning they would be both sad and happy. Understandably shaken, they obeyed the voice and traveled on through the rest of the night without stopping. When morning dawned, these three merchants anxiously looked into their pockets. Instead of finding the pebbles as expected, there were precious jewels! And, they were both happy and sad. Happy that they had picked up some of the pebbles, but sad because they hadn't gathered more when they had the opportunity.

This fable expresses how many of us feel about the treasures of God's Word. There is coming a day when we will be thrilled because we have absorbed as much as we have, but sad because we had not gleaned much more. Jewels are best shown off when held up to a bright light and slowly turned so that each polished facet can catch and reflect the light.

Each of these nine jewels of character will be examined in the light of God's Word and how best to allow them to be developed in the individual life. That is how I feel about the following three verses from Paul's writings which challenge us with what their Christian character or personality should look like. Jesus Christ has boiled down a Christian's responsibility to two succinct commands: Love the Lord your God with all your heart, mind, soul, and body, and love your neighbor like yourself. Likewise, Paul the apostle has captured for us the Christian personality in nine traits:

> But the fruit of the Spirit is love, joy, peace, patience, kindness, goodness, faithfulness, gentleness, and self-control. Against such things there is no law. Those who belong to Christ Jesus have crucified the sinful nature with its passions and desires. Since we live by the Spirit, let us keep in step with the Spirit (Gal. 5:22–25).

At the very beginning of this study, I must point out a subtle, yet obvious, distinction. The "fruit" of the Spirit is a composite description of what the Christian lifestyle and character traits are all about — an unbroken whole. We can't pick only the fruit we like.

Unlocked in these nine portraits are the riches of a Christ-centered personality. The thrill of the search is ahead of us!

Patience

MAKROTHUMIA, (Greek)
pronounced mak-roth-oo-meh'-ah, meaning:
forbearance, long-enduring, fortitude,
long-suffering, and patience.

THE FRUIT OF THE
SPIRIT IS . . . PATIENCE

Have you ever exclaimed or prayed: "Lord, I want patience and I want it right now!"? What we have failed to recognize is that the Lord has been patiently waiting to give us patience long before

> *Lack of patience can poison relationships and too often ruins what would otherwise be wonderful and maybe even brilliant personalities.*

we even thought of asking for it. God doesn't have to try to be patient — He is! I'm so thankful that He is patient with us through all of our ups and downs, our ins and outs. Of all of the fruit of the Spirit, it's easier to joke about patience than it is to become a patient person.

Before we get too far into this study, I must make a confession. I am not an expert on this subject. I'm still learning. It's still a process over which there is a lot of struggle going on. Patience is something I have to continually keep working on. Too often there is a churning going on inside. So if you understand this, perhaps we will be fellow learners, fellow travelers. All of us are still in search of more patience, especially how to develop a harvest of fruit called patience. The benefits of developing patience are more than worth the process and pain. So fellow Christian . . . let's embark on this study together.

When dealing with the subject at hand . . . have you learned of the Chinese bamboo tree? The Chinese plant the seed; water and fertilize it, but the first year nothing happens. The second year they water and fertilize it, and still nothing happens. No sign of life bursting through the earth. The third and fourth year they water and fertilize it . . . and sometime during the course of the fifth year, in a period of about six weeks, this bamboo tree grows to a height of approximately 90 feet!

The question is: Did it grow 90 feet in six weeks or did it grow 90 feet in five years? The obvious answer is that it took all of the five years because without the nurture and care of the preceding period of time, there would be no tree.

Now, another question: When does a person develop patience? At the point of the new birth? How long does it take to cultivate this fruit to maturity? What does it take to make the process happen?

The special application of this quality of character is most often exhibited in our dealing with other people — relationships. Perhaps it's easier to approach this from the negative side. Lack of patience can poison relationships and too often ruins what would otherwise be wonderful and maybe even brilliant personalities. We understand the opposite of patience is temper, shortness with other folk, and very destructive to long-lasting relationships.

When dealing with patience, we all must acknowledge it is the little things that seem to drive us to despair. The enemy of our souls doesn't often concentrate on the big battles but continuously pounds away at the little things. Because we are prepared to handle the big things, we fail to recognize the continued erosion going on. The unknown poet of the following has captured our threat and dilemma:

> I thought, if defeat came at all,
> It would be in a big, bold
> Definite joust
> With a cause or a name,
> And it came.
>
> I had not thought the daily skirmish
> With a few details, worthwhile;
> And so I turned my back upon them
> Year on year; until one day
> A million minutias blanketed together
> Rose up and overwhelmed me.

Oh, how elusive patience can become. And just think of all the little enemies we deal with on a daily basis that do all within their power to destroy any vestige of patience we might have or have attempted to cultivate. In the natural . . . the cultivation of the fruit of patience is well nigh impossible. How do I know that? Because I have attempted it without the help of the Spirit at work within. We are so vulnerable to these little foxes that are spoiling the vines. But do not despair completely! There is hope! Real hope! It's found in the Word of God. So let's begin. . . .

When Paul writes about this, the word "long-suffering" may have been more appropriate in his case. It could best have been defined as "endurance" in all situations.

> And we pray this in order that you may live a life worthy of the Lord and may please him in every way: BEARING FRUIT in every good work, growing in the knowledge of God, being

Theological Insight:

The Greek word for patience, makrothumia, *as used in verse 26, is interesting in its construction. The first half means "anger" and the other half means "long or slow." So we have the word meaning: "being able to handle one's anger slowly." Here is a major clue as to how patience is to be applied to interpersonal relationships.*

strengthened with all power according to his glorious might so that YOU may have great endurance and PATIENCE (Col. 1:10–11).

Phillips Brooks has captured the essence of Paul's challenge to his readers with these words: "Do not pray for easy lives; pray to be stronger men. Do not pray for tasks equal to your powers; pray for powers equal to your tasks. Then the doing of your work shall be no miracle, but you shall be a miracle. Every day you shall wonder at yourself, at the richness of life which has come to you by the grace of God."

THE RELATIONSHIP BETWEEN PATIENCE AND FORGIVENESS

We have already alluded to the importance of patience in relationships. The following study brings it into focus. In this portion of the Word, the teaching of Jesus points out how important it is that all good relationships with others must include patience as well as forgiveness and mercy. It's a cry that could be echoed from each with whom we have any kind of friendship, "Be patient with me. . . ."

Let's put that into a context by reading Matthew 18:21–35.

What is there in your relationships which causes you to become impatient with others?

_____

_____

_____

_____

_____

This portion begins with the well-known exchange between Peter and the Lord. "How many times shall I forgive?" is the question. How does forgiveness and patience inter-relate?

_____

_____

_____

_____

_____

_____

In this same chapter, verses 15–17 speak of another phase of relationships. But it seems as though the situation deals with a fellow Christian. Jesus said, "If your brother sins against you. . . ." Peter asked, "Lord, how many times shall I forgive my brother when he sins against me?" Why do you think this emphasis is so pointed toward the relationships with other Christians?

_____

_____

_____

_____

What did the first servant ask for from the king? Patience. Why do you think he didn't treat his fellow servant like he wanted to be treated?

_____

_____

_____

_____

_____

Is there to be a difference in the way we treat a brother or sister or fellow worker than we would treat a non-Christian? Please explain:

_____

_____

_____

_____

Do you think this story really happened or is it simply a parable to convey this truth?

_____

_____

_____

_____

How was the first servant's plea for patience rewarded?

_____

_____

_____

Why don't you think he was willing to be patient with his fellow servant and wait for the repayment?

_____

_____

_____

Did you notice that the interaction between these two servants was observed by other servants? Why were his actions causing such great distress?

_____

_____

_____

_____

Are you bothered when you see such injustices and impatience done to others? What can you do about such actions?

_____

_____

_____

In the light of verse 35, how important is it that we treat others with patience?

_____

_____

_____

_____

_____

_____

What does it mean to "forgive . . . from the heart?"

_____

_____

_____

_____

_____

_____

_____

 *ASSIGNMENT:*

• Think of someone to whom you have acted with impatience:

_____

_____

• What are the steps you can take to extend forgiveness as well as patience to mend that relationship?

_____

_____

_____

_____

PATIENCE IN ACTION

Have you ever been in a situation, in a strange place, where you are required to look for road signs as well as study a map to decipher where you are going? Did you drive slower than some of the native drivers? Did they honk at you, shake a fist, or worse, yell at you because you were going too slow? Sometimes . . . the going in the Christian life can be slow because we are entering into new territory. If we have walked down a particular valley and someone else is going through the same kind of test or trial, why can't we be more patient with them? It works both ways. Sometimes, perhaps too often, our responses to others are not as wonderful and godly as they should be. The Christian walk takes time to take care of others. It doesn't mean that we are not making progress . . . but we do it deliberately.

TEACH ME, LORD, TO WAIT

Lord, to wait down on my knees
Till in Your own good time You answer my pleas;
Teach me not to rely on what others do,
But to wait in prayer for an answer from You.

They that wait upon the Lord shall renew their
     strength,
They shall mount up with wings as eagles;
They shall run and not be weary,
They shall walk and not faint.
Teach me, Lord, teach me, Lord, to wait.
                    (Stuart Hamblen)

Just because you are waiting, exercising patience, doesn't mean you are passive. On the contrary, patience can be very active . . . when exercised it's a concentration of strength. It's more than simply enduring. It's a discipline at work moving us to a point that God has in mind. It's a robust, vigorous kind of thing being built on the fact that God is patience as well as being love.

Now, read the Scripture portion from James 1:12–27.

As we look at this first chapter of James, it's a single tapestry of truth woven about the concepts of trials and temptations, listening and doing. How do these things interrelate?

_____

_____

_____

_____

What does being "quick to listen" have to do with patience?

_____

_____

_____

What does "slow to speak" have to do with patience?

_____

_____

_____

_____

What does being "slow to become angry" have to do with patience?

_____

_____

_____

_____

What brings about the "righteous life that God desires"?

_____

_____

_____

_____

How are we to get rid of "all moral filth" and the "evil that is so prevalent"?

_____

_____

_____

_____

_____

_____

James, being the practitioner that he is, concentrated his attention on the "doing" as opposed to the "being." Does "doing" lead to "being" or does "being" lead to the correct actions of "doing"? Please explain:

_____

_____

_____

_____

_____

From verse 26, what does James mean by keeping "a tight rein" on the tongue?

_____

_____

_____

_____

How *can* a tight rein be kept on the tongue?

_____

_____

_____

How does keeping a tight rein on the tongue relate to patience?

_____

_____

_____

_____

How does "religion," which is accepted as "pure and faultless," behave?

_____

_____

_____

_____

How can a pure and faultless religion be attained?

_____

_____

_____

ASSIGNMENT:

• What in your own personal life which causes you to be impatient?

_____

_____

_____

• How could you slow down your pace in life in order to begin living the patient lifestyle of the Word?

_____

_____

_____

_____

_____

_____

PATIENCE AND SOME RULES FOR HOLY LIVING

PATIENCE is the guardian of faith, the preserver of peace, the cherisher of love, the teacher of humility. PATIENCE governs the flesh, strengthens the spirit, sweetens the temper, stifles anger, extinguishes envy, subdues pride: she bridles the tongue, restrains the hand, tramples upon temptations, endures persecutions, consummates martyrdom.

*Therefore . . .
clothe yourselves
with compassion,
kindness, humility,
gentleness and
patience. Bear with
each other and
forgive whatever
grievances you may
have against one
another. Forgive as
the Lord forgave you
(Col. 3:12–13).*

PATIENCE produces unity in the church, loyalty in the state, harmony in families and society; she comforts the poor, and moderates the rich; she makes us humble in prosperity, cheerful in adversity, unmoved by calamity and reproach; she teaches us to forgive those who have injured us, and to be the first in asking forgiveness of those whom we have injured; she delights the faithful, and invites the unbelieving; she adorns the woman and approves the man; she is beautiful in either sex and every age. Behold her appearance and her attire![1]

Now, that is said well. Patience is the character virtue that enables all the others to develop and mature. Without patience, nothing that takes time could happen, including character development and the harvest of the Spirit in each believer's spirit.

Patience is a transcending kind of virtue. It's inter-related with the rules and plans of God for mature, daily living that stands the test of time. Again, I remind you that this is the character trait that God wants to bestow and develop in each of us.

With this as our background, our next study comes from Colossians 3:1–17.

In the first four verses, Paul writes about our part in mature living. What does it mean to "set your heart on things above"?

_____

_____

_____

_____

_____

_____

What does it mean to "set your mind on things above"?

_____

_____

_____

_____

According to verse 5, how are you to "put to death . . . whatever belongs to your earthly nature"?

_____

_____

_____

Why is it so necessary for us to put off these things before we put on a new self?

_____

_____

_____

_____

In verse 11, Paul puts to rest once and for all any distinctions in the body of Christ. What relationship does this have with developing patience?

_____

_____

_____

_____

What does it mean to "God's chosen people"?

_____

_____

_____

How are we/you to "clothe" ourselves with compassion?

_____

_____

_____

_____

Kindness?

_____

_____

_____

_____

Humility?

_____

_____

_____

_____

Gentleness?

_____

_____

_____

_____

Patience?

_____

_____

_____

_____

What does "bear with each other" have to do with patience?

_____

_____

_____

_____

How can we achieve "perfect unity"?

_____

_____

_____

_____

How are we to "let the peace of Christ rule in our hearts"?

_____

_____

_____

_____

How are we to "let the word of Christ dwell in you"?

_____

_____

_____

_____

What does the bottom-line (verse 17) say to you?

_____

_____

_____

_____

 *ASSIGNMENT:*

• What is the major theme of this study for your life?

_____

_____

_____

_____

How will you make it a life application?

_____

_____

_____

_____

• Is there a person in your life at this moment with whom you need to show more patience?

_____

_____

Explain exactly how you plan to do this:

_____

_____

_____

_____

PATIENCE, SUFFERING, AND PERSEVERANCE

I don't like to wait for anything! How about you? Do you like to wait? Waiting in lines, waiting for a long-expected letter, waiting for a promised check, waiting for someone, waiting for some important piece of information, waiting on slow people, waiting for a special appointment . . . all of these seem to bother me. But are they real problems? No . . . merely an inconvenience.

But waiting can be a much more serious situation . . . waiting for God to answer a prayer for guidance, waiting for that special person for marriage, waiting for the dreaded report from the doctor, waiting and hoping for a breakthrough in a career, waiting out a serious illness, waiting anxiously as a student who has completed college for that first real job. These and other kinds of waiting are the focus in this section of our study.

> There's no music in a "rest," but there's the making of music in it. And people are always missing that part of the life melody, always talking of perseverance and courage and fortitude; but patience is the finest and worthiest part of fortitude, and the rarest, too.[2]

Our study now takes us into the Old Testament as well as the New Testament. Let's read Psalm 40:1–7 and James 5:7–12.

What is it about waiting that is so difficult for you?

_____

_____

_____

_____

Be patient, then, brothers, until the Lord's coming. . . . You too, be patient and stand firm, because the Lord's coming is near (James 5:7–8).

Can you think of a time and situation in your life when you were waiting on God?

_____

_____

_____

David writes, "I waited PATIENTLY for the Lord." What is the difference between waiting "patiently" and waiting "impatiently"?

_____

_____

_____

_____

In your life . . . why is waiting patiently for the Lord such a tough assignment?

_____

_____

_____

What were the benefits which God provided to David as a result of his patiently waiting upon God?

_____

_____

_____

_____

_____

Explain how verse 8, "I desire to do your will," is related to being able to wait patiently:

_____

_____

_____

_____

_____

From James 5:7, how long are we to be patient?

_____

_____

_____

_____

How is developing patience much like the farmer and his crops?

_____

_____

_____

_____

What is "grumbling"?

_____

_____

_____

_____

And why are we not to "grumble against each other"?

_____

_____

_____

_____

How is not grumbling related to patience?

_____

_____

_____

_____

Why are the "prophets" such an example of patience?

_____

_____

_____

_____

Why was Job such an example of perseverance?

_____

_____

_____

_____

What does the Lord being "full of compassion and mercy" have to do with our patience, suffering, and perseverance?

_____

_____

_____

_____

 ASSIGNMENT:

• David was a man who celebrated his victories by writing new songs extolling God and God's help in his life. Maybe you have never done anything like this, but how about writing a few lines of expression to praise God for His working in your life? You can do it! Just begin and let it flow.

_____

_____

_____

_____

• How will you apply the practical lesson from James to your lifestyle?

_____

_____

_____

_____

PATIENCE UNTO THE VERY END

The Holy Spirit produces patience in a believer by the simple method of giving something to endure or to wait for. Patience,

In the ultimate test of patience, it's a waiting for future glory, a waiting for heaven's reward, it's a waiting until death takes us home.

when you stop and think about it, will not be produced in any other method. People who have nothing to endure, nothing to wait for, nothing to persevere through, nothing that requires a long-haul commitment will not easily manifest this genuine harvest of the Spirit. With patience . . . the coming of the harvest may seem slow and may never appear in this lifetime. It's a life-long school into which we have been enrolled. Patience is simply suffering long or "long-suffering" as the King James Version tells us. The obvious sometimes seems elusive. In the ultimate test of patience, it's a waiting for future glory, a waiting for heaven's reward, it's a waiting until death takes us home.

This particular focus of study is captured for us in these words: "Be patient, then . . . until the Lord's coming" (James 5:7). This exercise in patience is not apparently that easy because the apostle Peter has words of encouragement about the passing of time until this event happens. It's a major recurring theme of the Lord and His followers. Wait . . . be patient . . . it will happen . . . until then, live a worthy life . . . don't despair or give up hope. Use this wait to be productive, develop the characteristic of patience because it will be rewarded.

> Let nothing disturb thee;
> Let nothing dismay thee:
> All things pass;
> God never changes.
> Patience attains
> All that it strives for.
> He who has God
> Finds he lacks nothing:
> God alone suffices.
> (St. Teresa of Avila)

All of life is composed of waiting periods. The child must wait until he is finally old enough to ride a bicycle . . . the young man anxiously waits until he is finally old enough to get a license so he can drive a car . . . for the college student there is a wait until the diploma is earned . . . the manager waits for that hard-earned promotion . . . the young couple waits out the nine months until their child is born . . . and on and on. But the waiting until the end may be the hardest and longest of all waits.

Our study for this section is found in 2 Peter 3:1–15; Matthew 10:22; and Romans 8:18–25.

Why do you think Peter wrote this warning in his second letter?

_____

_____

_____

_____

What is this "coming" he is talking about?

_____

_____

_____

_____

Do you think Peter had a literal meaning in mind when he wrote, "With the Lord a day is like a thousand years, and a thousand years are like a day"? Or is he simply using a figure of speech? Explain:

_____

_____

_____

_____

Why, according to verse 9, is the Lord so patient?

_____

_____

_____

_____

In the light of the coming "day of the Lord," what kind of a lifestyle should we as Christians be living?

_____

_____

_____

From Matthew 10:22, exactly what is Jesus referring to?

_____

_____

_____

_____

Why?

_____

_____

_____

_____

Is this same "end" that Peter has written about?

_____

_____

_____

_____

Now read Romans 8:18–25. Would you compare "our present sufferings" to "the glory" which is to come:

_____

_____

_____

_____

What "creation" waits for "the sons of God to be revealed"?

_____

_____

_____

Do you think, in verse 23, that the "first fruits" have any kind of reference to the fruit of the Spirit being developed with each of us? Please explain:

_____

_____

_____

Exactly what is this "hope" to which he refers?

_____

_____

_____

_____

_____

Paul uses all kinds of "family" words in this section . . . such as "sons" or "children," etc. Please go back through this passage and list them:

_____

_____

_____

_____

_____

What are these terms conveying to you about patience and our future as Christians?

_____

_____

_____

_____

_____

This is beyond our study text, but read Romans 8:28–30. Now explain how these words of comfort relate to our waiting patiently:

_____

_____

_____

_____

_____

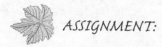 *ASSIGNMENT:*

• Please write out the lessons on patience you have learned from the Word in this study:

_____

_____

_____

_____

_____

_____

• How will you be applying these truths to your daily living?

_____

_____

_____

_____

_____

IN SUMMARY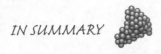

Some of the hardest life-lessons involve learning patience. To learn to wait while your child in the high chair does everything with his food but eat it. To be willing to quietly sit and listen as a long-winded friend bores you yet again with another of those endless stories. To be ready to actively listen as your child talks in aggravatingly minute details about everything that happened in her day.

To be patient without interrupting. To be patient while standing in the checkout line behind an elderly person carefully counting out his exact change for a purchase. To not explode at the driver in front of you. To be able to quiet the impulse to shout. To be able to curb anger when you are wronged. The song-writer penned such a simple line, "Oh what peace we often forfeit. . . ." By living life in a hurried frenzy, careening out of control and exhibiting anger at others, we live the opposite of the life example Jesus Christ set before us. Oh, to be patient! What a tough lesson to learn because it's tested nearly every day by little as well as big things over which we have no control!

Waiting is not high on the list of things to do in our hurry-up world. Patience has never been a strength of the human flesh. But that doesn't change a thing. The Bible is full of things to say about waiting. Let's take the time to sample a few more of these gems of truth.

No one whose hope is in you will ever be put to shame (Ps. 25:3).

Guide me in your truth and teach me, for you are God my Savior, and my hope is in you all day long (Ps. 25:5).

Wait for the Lord; be strong and take heart and wait for the Lord (Ps. 27:14).

In your name I will hope, for your name is good (Ps. 52:9).

My soul finds rest in God alone (Ps. 62:1).

Find rest, O my soul, in God alone; my hope comes from Him (Ps. 62:5).

Those who hope in the Lord will renew their strength (Isa. 40:31).

So do not throw away your confidence; it will be richly rewarded. You need to persevere so that when you have done the will of God, you will receive what he has promised (Heb. 10:35–36).

Yet the Lord longs to be gracious to you; He rises to show you compassion. For the Lord is a God of justice. Blessed are all who wait for him! (Isa. 30:18).

If God wasn't in the business of maturing His children, the process wouldn't take nearly so long. He is always more interested in our growth than He is in our getting our every want, whim, and wish. Therefore, waiting is a most useful tool that is essential when you consider the end result. He is not into the "instant" anything kind of convenience, especially when it comes to growing sons and daughters prepared for the Kingdom.

So what do you do when you are waiting? At least you can know this — it has a purpose. Know also that He is not tantalizing or teasing you. He is not testing you beyond what you can endure. He takes no great delight in making you wait. He has a total person in view, a mature

By living life in a hurried frenzy, careening out of control and exhibiting anger at others, we live the opposite of the life example Jesus Christ set before us.

person. He doesn't want you to fail in this process. He doesn't want you to drown before you have learned how to swim. REST . . . RELAX in Him and the goodness of God. It may seem as though nothing is happening but in reality something is in process. Keep the faith, hold on to your hope, endure to the end, and don't give up on yourself or His working in your life.

There is no way to teach or preach patience into people. You will never learn these lessons until you are subjected to the give-and-take as well as the rough-and-tumble of the real world out there.

I have no idea whether the following story is true or not . . . it sounds plausible and it has a powerful message.

ONE MORE TIME

Rafael Solano was physically exhausted and defeated. He sat on a boulder in the dry riverbed and announced to his crew, "I'm through. There's no use going on any longer. See this pebble? It makes 999,999 I've picked up without finding one diamond. One more pebble makes a million, but what's the use? I quit!"

This took place in 1942. This exploration crew had spent months prospecting for diamonds in a Venezuelan riverbed and watercourse. Their efforts were focused on finding signs of a valuable diamond field. Mentally, physically, and emotionally they were exhausted. Their clothes were in tatters and their spirits ready to quit. "Pick up just one more and make it an even million," one crew member said. Solano nodded and went back into the riverbed and pulled up a stone about the size of a hen's egg. It was different than the others, and the crew soon discovered it was a diamond! It was later sold to Harry Winston, a New York diamond dealer. That millionth pebble was named the "Liberator" and to date is supposedly the largest and purest diamond ever found.

You may have become discouraged with your progress in patience! Don't give up no matter how many times you have tried and failed. With God's help, let's go after it one more time. Harriet Beecher Stowe said, "Never give up, for that is just the place and time that the tide will turn."

Rafael Solano would agree with that. Now, my friend, how about you? It's too soon to give up on patience in your life.

Have patience with all things, but chiefly have patience with yourself.

Never give up, for that is just the place and time that the tide will turn.
(Harriet Beecher Stowe)

Do not lose courage in considering your imperfections, but instantly set about remedying them . . . every day begin the task anew. (St. Francis de Sales)

Wherefore seeing we also are compassed about with so great a cloud of witnesses, let us lay aside every weight, and the sin which doth so easily beset [us], AND LET US RUN WITH PATIENCE the race that is set before us, Looking unto Jesus the author and finisher of [our] faith. . . . that endured such contradiction of sinners against himself, lest ye be wearied and faint in your minds (Heb. 12:1–3; KJV).

And the fruit of the spirit is . . . PATIENCE!

1   Bishop Horne, *6,000 Sermon Illustrations* (Grand Rapids, MI: Baker Book House, 1956).
2   Ruskin, *The New Dictionary of Thoughts*.

Nine Fruits of the Spirit

Study Series includes

Love

Joy

Peace

Patience

Kindness

Goodness

Faithfulness

Gentleness

Self-Control

Robert Strand

Retired from a 40-year ministry career with the Assemblies of God, this "pastor's pastor" is adding to his reputation as a prolific author. The creator of the fabulously successful Moments to Give series (over one million in print), Strand travels extensively, gathering research for his books and mentoring pastors. He and his wife, Donna, live in Springfield, Missouri. They have four children.

Rev. Strand is a graduate of North Central Bible College with a degree in theology.